MW01061578

Introduction

Failure is such a miserable thing. When it appears in one's life, it can do lasting damage to self-esteem and confidence. Nobody respects or celebrates a "loser". We have all felt the emotional heaviness that comes upon us when defeat darkens our doorstep.

So called success on the other hand is always celebrated and admired. The successful people in life whatever their field of endeavor – are lifted up as idols, to be worshipped and emulated.

And as much as failure is feared and success is craved, neither is truly understood unless seen through the eyes of a lifetime. When Richard Nixon died in 1994, President Bill Clinton gave the eulogy.

He said something that I have never forgotten. When pondering the many triumphs and tragedies of Nixon's life he simply said......

"Sometimes you can't fully measure a tree until it's down".

Success and failure are cousins, if not siblings. You really can't have one without the other.

I have often observed that we humans seem to lack the "big picture" – namely the ability to see beyond three inches in front of our face. There are many reasons for this but the major one is that we are only on this Earth for 80-90 years (if we are lucky) and we often don't have the ability to see the complete picture of a lifetime of work and effort.

We judge ourselves like one trick ponies. If we embark on an adventure and it bombs, we consider ourselves a failure – forever. We often feel that if we are not successful at everything we try (or we don't nail it the first time), we label ourselves as defective.

Over the years, I have studied the lives of some incredibly successful people. Time and time again, these individuals were not destined for greatness. Many of them started out dirt poor, uneducated, some practically illiterate and often seen as outcasts by the people of their time.

In fact, many now iconic people had a lot of failure in life. Some would even say that they failed many more times than they succeeded. But the one main trait that ran through all of them was that they never gave up. They never let defeat stop them or allow their circumstances to define them. In short, they never stopped trying until they made it

I wrote this book for both you and me. The stories contained here are about people who changed the world while still having their fair share of failure, setbacks and less than ideal conditions from which to start. In the end, they were all very human – just like us. If one person reading this book fully accepts and internalizes that they are no different from these iconic legends then its writing will have been worthwhile. For in the end, life truly plays no favorites.

Chapter One:

Thomas Alva Edison

"I haven't failed, I just found 1000 ways that won't work"

In the history of the modern world, there will never again be a Tom Edison. He is responsible for so many of the conveniences of life today, the light bulb being only one of them. He literally brought man from a world of candles and darkness to one of illumination. It is unthinkable to a modern person to survive without his many inventions. To read a list of the other innovations that he directly developed or had a material hand in is nothing short of unbelievable.

In addition to the first long lasting, functional light bulb, Thomas Edison also developed the phonograph, the motion picture camera, the first electronic vote recording machine and a device to separate iron ore. Such innovations were unheard of until he set his mind to work on overcoming the obstacles that prevented such products from being developed.

And while in later life and in death, Edison was celebrated as the great genius of his time, his life didn't start out destined for greatness.

Edison's middle name was Alva – Hence he was called "Little Al" during a period of his young childhood. He was the last of seven siblings. He didn't talk until he was nearly four years old. Today, many medical experts would term this condition as being "delayed" or perhaps even cognitively impaired.

However once he did start communicating, he would constantly ask adults "why" when exposed to the workings of any device or idea that he came across. Contrary to folklore, Thomas Edison was not born into a poor family. Born February 11th, 1847, his parents were well established within the middle class of Milan Ohio. During the time of his birth, Milan was one of the world's largest shippers of wheat.

In 1854 at the age of seven, the Edison family moved to Port Huron, Michigan, which also had a very strong commercial presence. During this time, young Tom also started school. He was enrolled in a one room school house that contained a total of 38 students of all ages.

The teacher at the school was often described as overworked and suffered from a short temper. Managing children of so many different ages and levels proved very taxing for this particular instructor.

Young Edison brought with him to school his ever-expanding insatiable curiosity and a near lust for knowledge. Tom's persistent questioning of his teacher was considered arrogant and self-centered. He was seen as a distraction to the other students and he often would throw the teacher off of his class plans for the day.

Finally after spending only 12 weeks in the noisy, one-room school house, the teacher's patience with Little Al Edison wore thin. The instructor finally could hold back no longer. He was willing to share his opinion of Tom Edison with whoever would listen. One of his first observations was that Edison's physical appearance was clearly influenced by his cognitive limitations.

Noting that Tom's forehead was very broad and his head seem to be extremely large, the teacher who taught the boy who would go on to change the world could only conclude that young Tom's brain had to be "addled".

The term "addled" was a common one in the 19th Century to describe someone who "just wasn't right". If modern medicine had been in existence back then, Thomas Edison would have been deemed "mentally retarded" or "slow". Even in today's politically correct environment, he would have been labeled "impaired".

Despite this very tough start to his formal education, Edison flourished as a youth. When asked about it, he always gave the credit to his mother, Nancy for never giving up on him. He was often quoted that his mother "was the making of me because she was always so true and so sure of me".

His mother's confidence in him fueled his sense of a purpose for his life. He would later say that he felt an obligation to never disappoint her. Once his formal schooling days were over, his mother began to home school young Tom. Despite being labeled as "addled" by the officials at the school, young Edison became enthralled with history and literature under his mother's instruction. In fact, he took a particular interest in Shakespeare. His parents soon exposed him to the Library and taught him how to utilize the resources there. He soon absorbed the classics in science and literature.

As his teen and early adulthood years came upon him, Tom became very entrepreneurial. He became a very successful salesman of newspapers and other items on board trains. He also developed into a very astute telegraph operator and traveled all over the country. But life was just beginning for the young Edison. During these years, Edison also developed very severe hearing problems that eventually later in life would render him nearly completely deaf. He would struggle with his hearing from early adulthood onward.

THE INVENTION OF THE LIGHT BULB

Today it is inconceivable to live in a world without light bulbs. Our whole civilization is based on our reliance of artificial light. But much to our surprise, light bulbs didn't always exist. In fact it's amazing that we have only had electric lights in common use for the past 135 years. It is also a common myth that Thomas Edison invented the light bulb. He actually didn't. He was not the first one nor the only person trying to perfect the incandescent light bulb.

Early inventions of the light bulb go back as far as 1802. During the 1840's, and beyond, scientists in other parts of the world continued their research on perfecting artificial, electric light. Actually the name of Edison's first light patent in 1878 was filed under "Improvement in Electric Lights". While early experimenters with the light bulb did make progress, a common problem had to do with the lights burning out very quickly.

During peoples' years of experimentation, many different types of metals and other materials were put into a bulb (under a vacuum) and electricity was passed through it. While these prototypes did produce a glowing light, they burned out and failed in a very short time. Some of them were also made from very expensive materials, rendering them impractical for mass or commercial production. By 1879, Edison had filed another patent that contained the description of his most effective discovery – the use of "a carbon filament or strip coiled and connected."

Other materials were described as well such as the use of "cotton and linen thread, wood splints, papers coiled in various ways." So really what Edison did was invent the first long lasting, commercially viable light bulb that could be mass produced in an economical way.

People interested in history know that Edison's perfecting the light bulb was certainly not an overnight success. The truth of the matter is that he failed again and again in his ability to make the light bulb burn a sufficient amount of time to make its use worthwhile. In fact, it is said that Edison failed between 600- 1000 times to get a bulb that would not burn out too quickly. In typical Edison fashion, the great inventor said....

"I didn't fail 1000 times to make the light bulb work, I just discovered 1000 ways that it didn't work".

Of all the great inventions of the modern age, the story of Thomas Edison and the light bulb is one of the best illustrations of never giving up, remaining hopeful and always seeking a solution to a given problem no matter what.

EDISON'S REACTION TO THE LAB FIRE OF 1914

Here is another amazing example of the character and vision of Thomas Edison. On December 9th, 1914 a huge explosion and fire occurred in one of the buildings of Edison's West Orange New Jersey Laboratory buildings. Many nearby buildings were destroyed as well. The damage was in excess of 7 million dollars. The affected buildings were insured for less than $250,000 due to the fact that they were made of concrete and were thought to be quite incapable of burning.

Years of work and hundreds of experiments were destroyed in the fire. As the 67 year old Edison stood with his family and watched the destruction, he remarked:

"There is great value in destruction – all of our mistakes burned up. It doesn't matter – I'll start anew tomorrow morning." He rented space in other facilities and within weeks, his operations were back to near normal productivity levels. This kind of setback would have devastated most people. But not Edison. He believed in moving forward no matter what obstacles or circumstances fell upon him.

Let us continue to fully realize that Thomas Edison was just as human and subject to uncontrollable conditions just as any other person. We can all learn and be inspired by the life of this great American.

Chapter Two:

Henry Ford

"Men never fail, they just stop trying"

Of all the famous people throughout time, very few stand out more than Henry Ford. It could be said very easily that he was the "father of the 20th Century". Perhaps more than any other person of his time, he brought the world into the modern age. His beloved Model T automobile changed the lives of millions of people. The Model T was the first automobile that was massed produced to the extent that common people could afford to own one. Prior to the Model T, the automobile was a toy that only rich people could afford to acquire. The inexpensive, durable and charming "Tin Lizzy" opened up the country and the world to the motoring public. From 1908 to 1927, over 15 million Model T's were produced. In fact at one time during the 1920's over 50% of the automobiles on the road were Model T's.

The lessons to be learned by the life of Henry Ford are wonderfully numerous. Many people falsely believe that Henry Ford invented the automobile, the production line or the gasoline powered engine. None of these are actually true. Like so many people who have had a profound impact on the world, life was not always so rosy for Henry Ford. In fact, he had many setbacks and even tragedy beset him early on. But like so many influential people, he used his failures and losses to motivate him to never give up and persevere until successful.

Henry Ford was born in July 1863 on a farm in Michigan. His father was an immigrant from Ireland with British heritage. He had four siblings and was the oldest child. Like many children of the mid to late 19th Century, Henry's formal education was spotty to say the least. In fact, Ford stayed somewhat illiterate his whole life. He could function but clearly his spelling and grammar skills left much to be desired. During his early years, it was clear that young Henry had a natural ability for all things mechanical.

Like many young boys, he began to tinker with things and loved to take items apart to see how they worked. He started doing this with pocket watches. Many young men took apart pocket watches back then, but Henry Ford could actually put them back together and make them run. Life on the family farm was not easy and young Henry saw his father engage in heavy physical labor as a regular activity. Witnessing the struggles of 19th Century farming would stay with Henry Ford and later inspire him to design machines and other tools to "take the drudgery" out of physical work. His philosophy was simple. Never do again by hand what a machine could do for you.

At the age of 13, Henry Ford's mother died. This loss was a tragic blow to the young man. He loved his mother deeply and mourned her loss profoundly. Historians have noted that his mother's death surely caused the young Ford to mature beyond his years much quicker than most youth.

Shortly after his mother's death, he and his father were on the way to town in a horse drawn wagon.

A great hissing and clanging sound soon penetrated the air around them. The two Fords could see an enormous contraption coming toward them. It was one of the early 19th Century steam powered farm tractors that some of the well to do farmers had begun using. These machines resembled a small locomotive.

The sight of this monstrosity of a machine excited the young Ford beyond description. It was like a spiritual experience, a sort of a "road to Damascus" moment. At that exact moment, Henry Ford had caught the self- propelled machine "bug". He would spend the rest of his life pursuing the art of the machine.

Despite his new found inspiration for machinery, Henry Ford's road to success was not a quick one.

In fact, it took him quite a few years to get there. Ford's father had expected him to take over the family farm. But Henry was not really interested in that. He actually hated the intense physical labor associated with farming in the 19th Century.

At the age of 16, the young Henry left the family farm to take a job as an apprentice machinist in Detroit. He learned a great deal but that job didn't work out as well as he had hoped. He returned to the family farm at the age of 19. He then took a job repairing Westinghouse portable steam engines, something in which he had become an expert. But the world still didn't have any idea who Henry Ford was.

At the age of 25 he married the sister of a good friend. Her name was Clara Bryant. At the time of his marriage he was farming and running a saw mill. Their only son Edsel was born in 1891.

1891 was also the year that Henry Ford finally begun the road to his fateful place in history. But it was not a straight path to fame and fortune. During that year, Ford went to work for the Edison Illuminating Company and by 1893 was a Chief Engineer. It's important to keep in mind that for the previous decade before this time, Henry Ford had no real planned direction or progression for his life. He took it as it came.

After becoming Chief Engineer for the Edison organization, Ford began experimenting with his own versions of gasoline engines. On Christmas Eve 1893 as Mrs. Ford was preparing the Holiday turkey, stuffing and gravy, Henry Ford rushed into the kitchen with his just completed and first internal combustion engine. Precariously plugging it into the overhead light socket (for ignition), he set his wife upon the task of dripping gas into the crude engine. It fired up and soon began to fill the little kitchen up with smoke. An extremely joyful but oblivious Henry Ford gazed happily at his new found success.

For the man who would change the world with the production of fifteen million Model T's, success didn't initially come quickly. Ford would experiment for another 3 years with various types of engines before making his first automobile.

In 1896, Henry Ford had built his first car. It was called the "Quadricycle" as it was fashioned from a crude frame and 4 bicycle tires. His first vehicle had a four horse power engine with a 3 gallon fuel tank.

On June 4th 1896, the future automobile giant and an assistant were getting ready to take the world's first Ford out for a test run. One problem arose. The motor powered buggy was too wide to exit the shed in which it was built. Henry Ford soon solved that problem by taking an axe to one of the brick walls. After some noise and commotion, the new Ford was ready to hit the street.

The world premiere of Ford number one was by no means met with any fanfare. In fact, nobody noticed it at all. The car had two forward speeds but Henry couldn't shift it into second and it had no reverse. Hardly a glamorous beginning for the man who would mold the 20thcentury. But it was a start and Henry Ford had a date with destiny. It would be another two years before Henry Ford produced his second car. Often time great things start small and take struggle and effort.

Three years after his first automobile, Henry Ford (with some other investors) formed the Detroit Automobile Company. He was certainly not a pioneer at that time by starting a car company. Many automobile manufactures were springing up at that time – most of them now forgotten by history. During the early 1900's about one hundred automobile makers existed.

The new Detroit Automobile Company earnestly began their marketing efforts. But as it turned out, the cars they produced were much more expensive than Ford had wanted and of a much lower quality. In 1900 they had manufactured a delivery truck but it proved to be slow, unreliable and expensive to build. Sales never got off of the ground and the company wound up failing by 1901. Ford later recalled that the company's investors were more concerned with profit rather than innovation. This was a bitter but powerful lesson for the future industry leader.

After a successful period of racing early automobiles, another group joined Henry Ford and reformed the now defunct Detroit Automobile Company in 1901. They renamed it the Henry Ford Company, with Ford being the chief engineer. Ford was determined not to make the same mistakes again with this company. His goal was high quality but inexpensive cars. But once again, this was not to come to pass.

Soon after their earnest start, Ford had several significant disagreements with some of the financial backers and left the company in 1902. Ironically the company would eventually become Cadillac. Later that same year, Ford formed another partnership to make cars called "Ford and Malcomson Ltd". Again the goal was to produce inexpensive but quality made vehicles. Ford contracted with the Dodge Brothers for machining services. The Dodge Brothers soon demanded a huge payment up front before shipping their products and the new partnership was in jeopardy.

In response to this, Malcomson brought in some additional investors and convinced the Dodge Brothers to accept a portion of company ownership. On June 16th 1903, the Ford Motor Company was born.

Henry Ford was 40 years old that year.

The three time auto failure was about to embark on an adventure that would shape the 20th Century. It is very worthwhile to note that seven years had passed between Ford's first car (1896) and the formation of the Ford Motor Company in 1903. Certainly not an overnight success by any measurement.

THE LITTLE LIZZIE THAT CHANGED THE WORLD

It is not possible to overestimate the impact the Model T Ford had on the world. Debuting as a 1909 model (in the Fall of 1908), the Model T was inexpensive, well built, simple, rugged and the exact opposite of what most cars were at the time – expensive toys of the rich.

It is important to note also that the Model T did not come out until five years after the Ford Motor Company was established. Ford had experimented with a number of cars (starting with the Model A and working himself down the alphabet). His pre Model T cars were good and had modest success, but it was the Model T that changed it all. This new model was the realization of Henry Ford's long-time dream of building a low cost, high quality vehicle for the masses. The car opened up a new life for those who used them to travel to new destinations.

The Model T was the first car that the common person could afford to buy and operate. In 1913, Ford perfected the moving assembly line. Whereas at first it would take Ford employees 12.5 man hours to assemble a Model T – by the 1920's it only took 93 minutes to build a car.

In the 1920's over 50% of the cars on the road were Model T's. The Tin Lizzie (as it was affectionately known) was everywhere. On the street, in print and in movies. Even songs were written about people and their new Fords. From 1908 to 1927, over 15 million Model T's were produced. Henry Ford employed hundreds of thousands of people all over the world.

The Model T is the ancestor to every car on the road today. If you drove a car today, you can thank Henry Ford and the Model T. Most Model T's were melted down for World War Two but several hundred thousand still exist (including one owned by this author). They are very popular attractions at parades and car shows each year.

FAILURE AFTER SUCCESS -
THE EVENTUAL DEMISE OF THE MODEL T

When Model T production ended in May, 1927 Henry Ford had built over 15 million Tin Lizzies. The Model T literally opened the world to millions of people who had previously been stuck close to home with the horse and buggy as their only means of transport.

But then something happened. With 15 million Model T's in service, the demand for automobiles had begun to be met. During this time, a number of other prominent manufacturers started wide scale production themselves. By the late 1920's such companies as Chevrolet and Plymouth were marketing their line of cars to the American public. And these other companies realized that people were now looking for more than just basic transportation. Other brands started offering their cars in various different colors.

From 1917 until 1925 the Model T Ford came in only one color – Black. That was because Ford found that black paint dried the fastest on the assembly line. Starting in 1926 the Model T was offered in different colors but it was too late. The competition was making cars easier to drive and more comfortable with new available creature comforts that appealed to both taste and sense. The Model T had always been a crude but very dependable car and it was complicated to drive. It had multiple levers and pedals to work all at once. By 1926-27, the sales of the Model T were nowhere near what they had been even a few years before.

Henry Ford's son Edsel (1891-1943) had a flair for fashion and design. He finally convinced his father that if the Ford Motor Company was to survive, it was time to let go of the beloved Model T.

An almost fatal flaw of Henry Ford was that he was nearly unable to see that the Model T had run its course. This lack of perspective nearly drove the Ford Motor Company out of business. This is a very valuable lesson for us to learn from the Ford story. Just because something worked successfully for a good long time, it doesn't mean that the people and products involved don't need to change and grow over time.

Edsel got to work on the styling of the new car and Henry started on the mechanicals. In 1928, the completely new Model A hit the market and was a huge success. From 1928-1931, Ford sold 5 million Model A's. This new car was not a pioneer like the Model T had been but it was an up to date and fully modern car. The end of the Model T is an important lesson in flexibility and the willingness to accept change.

Chapter Three:

Abraham Lincoln

"Give me six hours to chop down a tree and I will spend the first four sharpening the axe".

So many books have been written on Abraham Lincoln that it boggles the mind. For most Americans, our earliest memories of our schooling are filled with images and lessons about our 16th President.

Most of us know the highlights of his life – that he came from humble beginnings, was a lawyer and presided over this nation during a crisis that was unprecedented at any time in history.

During Lincoln's presidency, the United States was embroiled in a bitter Civil War.

To this day, debates rage over the real "reason" for the Civil War. Most Northern people still say that the war was about the abolition of slavery and holding the union together. Many Southerners still believe in their hearts that the war was about State rights and the resistance against the overbearing power of the Federal Government. It is clear that even after 150 years since the war ended, the debate still has not been settled. People on both sides of the argument still hold very intense feelings about the issue. But what we do know today is that Abraham Lincoln saved this country from utter destruction. The fact that we today still exist as the United States of America is due to the efforts of this iconic leader.

But this chapter is not about the Civil War nor the lingering debate on the issue.

This chapter is about Abraham Lincoln – the man, the human being. Many people today do not know the full life story of Lincoln. And that life story had a lot of adversity and failure. Many are surprised when learning of all the losses and failure Lincoln suffered in his life time.

The road to iconic status was hardly guaranteed for Abraham Lincoln. It is only due to his unending drive (persistence) to press onward despite profound obstacles that he continues to live on in our hearts and minds more than 150 years after his death.

Abraham Lincoln was born in February 1809 in a Kentucky, one room wooden cabin. He was named after his grandfather, Captain Abraham Lincoln who was violently killed during an Indian raid in the late 1700's. Lincoln's father was a farmer and held other jobs such as cabinet maker and carpenter. Abraham was the middle child and had an older sister Nancy and a younger brother named Thomas. Thomas died in infancy.

During Lincoln's early life, his family became embroiled in several land title disputes, which resulted in the family's being uprooted from the farm in which they had been working.

Frustrated with the problems he encountered in Kentucky, Thomas Lincoln moved his family to Indiana. Young Abe would be just seven years old that year. Several profound events took place for Abraham Lincoln during his youth in Indiana. At the age of nine, Lincoln lost his mother. She had died of milk sickness, a common malady of the time. This time in history was long before the advent of pasteurization. His eleven year old sister Nancy would soon become the main caretaker of the home.

The following year (1819) Thomas Lincoln married Sarah "Sally" Bush Johnson. It wouldn't be long before young Abe grew very close to his stepmother. Lincoln's sister Nancy died in 1828 when he was only eighteen years old. He was very distraught by her death as he was very close to his big sister. Nancy died during childbirth and her son was stillborn.

Even though Lincoln's formal schooling probably wouldn't add up to a full year, the young man was very intellectually curious. He became an avid reader. He engrossed himself in books such as Aesop's Fables and others about the lives of Washington and Ben Franklin. He did not enjoy physical labor on the farm and many of his peers took him as "lazy" for preferring writing and reading.

He did perform his farm chores however with a firm character and a sense of responsibility.

During 1830-31, there was another milk-illness scare and the Lincolns decided to move to Illinois. By that time Abraham was about twenty two and was old enough to strike out on his own. Journeying by boat down the Sangamon River, Lincoln would wind up at the Village of New Salem, Illinois. New Salem was just outside of Springfield, the city in which he would later move to and live in until being elected President in 1860.

It is important to note that during the time of his arrival at New Salem, Lincoln had really no direction nor goals for his life. In fact he would say at the time "I am a piece of floating driftwood and I accidently landed at New Salem". Soon upon arriving, Lincoln was hired to pilot a flat boat down to New Orleans via the local river and the Mississippi. Upon arriving in New Orleans, Lincoln saw slavery for the first time and it would have a lasting impact on him.

Lincoln spent six years at New Salem. He would work a number of jobs including the co-owner of a general store (the Lincoln-Berry Store), postmaster, surveyor and rail splitter. Lincoln's time as a business man in New Salem wound up in failure and he was left with a considerable amount of debt.

He insisted on paying his debt off and it took years to accomplish this.

During his time at New Salem, Lincoln developed a romantic relationship with a woman named Ann Rutledge. He first met her upon his arrival and by 1835, he was deeply involved with her. He loved her very much but they had yet to become officially engaged. Historians feel that it was certainly Lincoln's intention to propose to her but it would never happen. In August of 1835, Ann passed away most likely of typhoid fever.

Lincoln was absolutely devastated by this loss. Ann had been the great love of his life.

Several historians have claimed that Lincoln had a nervous breakdown after the death of Ann Rutledge. In fact, some say that he spent 6 months in bed as a result.

The following year after Ann's death, Lincoln was courting a Kentucky woman named Mary Owens.

She came to New Salem but Lincoln and she had doubts about the wisdom of the relationship. Mary left the area and the courtship ended.

In December 1839, Lincoln met Mary Todd also of Kentucky. Mary was from a wealthy, slave holding family. Mary Todd and Abraham Lincoln could not have come from more different backgrounds.

Mary at times thought of Lincoln as being unsophisticated and unpolished. But she was taken with his folksy charm, wit and intelligence.

A year after meeting, Lincoln and Mary became engaged and were scheduled to be married in January, 1841. But the engagement was broken by him. They met up again and finally the romance was on for good. They were married at Springfield, IL in November 1842. During the preparation for the wedding, Lincoln continued to feel anxiety. When asked reflectively in which direction his life was heading, Lincoln simply said "To hell I suppose".

They purchased a one story home in Springfield in 1844. Mary Todd Lincoln was an out spoken woman who at times had the reputation of being very demanding and high maintenance. The Lincolns added a second story to the home and lived there until he was elected President in 1860. The original house still exists and is now operated by the National Park Service in Springfield.

Abraham and Mary Lincoln would have 4 boys during their marriage. Fate however would not be kind to the Lincoln children. Three of the four boys would die very young. Two of them before Lincoln's death and one shortly afterward. Only the oldest son, Robert Todd Lincoln would survive to live a normal life span and have children. Through the lineage of Robert Lincoln, the last direct descendant of Abraham Lincoln would live until 1985.

A few years before getting married, Lincoln tried his hand at elected office and suffered a great amount of defeat. While still at New Salem, he ran for the State Legislature. He finished eighth out of thirteen and was not elected. He would run again a short while later and was successful the second time.

As a newly-wed, he ran for U.S. Congress but was defeated. A few years later, he'd run again and was elected. But he would lose a bit for reelection.

During the 1850's, he ran for the U.S. Senate twice but was defeated. In 1856 he sought the Vice Presidential nomination but was unsuccessful. He would not get even one hundred votes. Of course Lincoln's fate as an icon was sealed when he was nominated for and won the Presidency in 1860.

Lincoln endured a tremendous amount of stress while serving as President during the Civil War. While in office, he lost a second son, Willie, to illness. His son Edward had died in 1850.

Abraham and Mary Lincoln grieved deeply over the death of Willie. Mary Todd Lincoln went into an almost catatonic depression after Willie passed away and would dress only in black for a long period of time. President Lincoln would have to learn to cope with their collective grief while at the same time leading the country during the Civil War.

It is often said that Presidents age extremely prematurely. Early photographs exist of Lincoln in both 1860 and 1865. The difference in appearance is shocking. When the Civil War ended in the Spring of 1865, it was a tremendous relief to Lincoln. Sadly, after surviving so much loss and adversity, he would only live for six days after Confederate General Robert E. Lee surrendered his army to the Union. Attending a play at Ford's Theater in Washington D.C. a jovial and at ease Lincoln would be shot in the head by John Wilkes Booth, a well known actor and Southern sympathizer. The 16th President of the United States would die the next morning.

ADVERSITY EVEN AFTER DEATH

Lincoln's relationship with adversity did not end upon his death. Lincoln died in 1865 and was not interred in his final resting place until 1901.

Upon his death, Lincoln was given a massive, national funeral. Travelling from Washington D.C to Springfield IL for burial, thousands and thousands of common ordinary people came to see his funeral train as it passed through their local area. When he had first died, interested parties had tried to approach Mrs. Lincoln about a proper burial site. In fact some had suggested that he be buried in an empty crypt in the Capitol Building that had been intended to be the final resting place of George Washington.

In the end, Mrs. Lincoln had insisted that he be buried in Oak Ridge Cemetery in Springfield.

When the funeral train left Washington D.C., it would contain both the bodies of Lincoln and his son Willie.

Upon arrival in Springfield, Lincoln's earthly remains were originally interred in a temporary vault while plans were made for a tomb to be built suitable for the martyred President. During the tomb planning stage, Lincoln's body would be moved multiple times between 1865 and 1901.

Adding insult to injury, Lincoln's body was nearly stolen on election night 1876. In fact, the only reason the theft was not successful was because the police were tipped off ahead of time and were present when the incident took place. The police actually allowed the thieves to get as far as lifting

Lincoln's coffin out of the vault in order to build a firm case against the grave robbers.

Finally in 1901, the Tomb was ready after having to be rebuilt the year before, due to its sinking into the ground. Lincoln was buried 10 feet underground, with a steel cage surrounding his coffin and vault. At the insistence of Robert Todd Lincoln (the only son to live to adulthood), thousands of pounds of concrete were poured into the cage and on top of the burial vault.

Because Lincoln's remains had been moved so many times prior to the 1901 final burial, it was suggested that the burial crew open the coffin just "to be safe" to confirm that the man they were burying under all the steel and concrete was indeed Abraham Lincoln.

When they opened the coffin for the last time, Lincoln looked completely recognizable. His hair, beard and facial mole were all very well preserved. It was concluded that he had been embalmed so many times in 1865 (during the train ride across the country) that his remains were amazingly intact.

President Abraham Lincoln was finally at peace. The last human being to actually lay eyes on Abraham Lincoln would live until 1963. Today Lincoln, his wife and 3 of his 4 sons are all buried in the same room at Oak Ridge Cemetery in Springfield. His oldest son, Robert Todd Lincoln is buried in Arlington National Cemetery.

Chapter Four:

Colonel Harland Sanders

"Don't quit at 65 for maybe your boat hasn't come in yet"

Who among us has not attended a picnic or a graduation party where Kentucky Fried Chicken was served? Doesn't it seem that there is a KFC on every corner in modern America? The image and face of Colonel Harland Sanders is very common. His picture conjures up a sweet, grandfatherly figure with his small white beard and matching white suit.

And while many of us know his chicken, few know the background of this American icon. For in reality, this hard working man had a life of some failure and adversity. In fact, he didn't even start Kentucky Fried Chicken until he was well into his 60's. When most people start thinking of retirement, Col Sanders was just getting started on his most famous adventure. His life story is an amazing tale of persistence and determination.

Harland Sanders was born in Indiana in September of 1890. He was the oldest of 3 children. His father Wilbur was a farmer and later a butcher. When young Harland was only five years old, his father came home one day with a fever. He was dead the next day. The family was devastated.

Reeling from her husband's death, Mrs. Sanders was forced to find work outside of the home. Five year old Harland (being the oldest) stepped up as best he could to take care of his two younger siblings. This environment was where his cooking skills began, trying to whip up meals for the kids while his mother was gone for days at a time trying to support the fatherless family. By the age of ten, Harland was working a job as a farm hand.

When he was twelve, his mother remarried but his relationship with his step father was a very bad one. It caused a great amount of stress in the young man's life. He would drop out of school at thirteen and went to work full time on a farm. He eventually secured a position as a street car conductor.

At the age of sixteen, he falsified his age and enlisted in the Army. After his stint in the military, the ever hard working youth supported himself in the railroad industry. First as a blacksmith's helper then an ash can cleaner and finally a fireman aboard the coal powered locomotives of the time. During this period on the railroad (at the age of nineteen) he met and married Miss Josephine King. They would have three children. A son and two daughters. His only son Harland Jr. died as a baby.

During his time after the military, he moved around from state to state. . He eventually lost his job on the railroad due to a brawl with a co-worker. Around this period, he was also studying law via a correspondence course. Sanders would practice law in Little Rock Arkansas but his legal career ended when he engaged in a court room fight with his own client.

In 1916 he got a job selling life insurance but was fired for insubordination. At the age of 30, he established a ferry boat company, which was an instant success. He would later sell his shares in that company to establish another business manufacturing acetylene lamps. However he was eventually driven out of business by the now famous organization, Delco, who at that time had pioneered the selling of their products on credit.

Moving into the ever growing automobile industry, he became a tire salesman. But that job ended when the manufacturing plant closed its doors. At the age of thirty four, he was running several gasoline service stations. But those facilities too closed once the Great Depression hit the country.

At forty, Shell Oil Company offered him the chance to run and manage a service station in North Corbin Kentucky. Having an idea to supplement the station's revenue, he began selling chicken, ham and steaks from the facility. He would later open an adjacent restaurant on the premises.

While running the gas station and restaurant, Sanders was actually involved in a gun shoot out in which one man was left dead on the street. The Sanders service station had a formidable competitor nearby. A man named Matt Stewart.

Stewart and Sanders were both hot tempered men. Sanders had put up a painted sign in the town to encourage customers to come to his Shell service station. Matt Stewart, the Standard Oil franchisee didn't take too kindly to the competitive advertising. Stewart had been caught trying to repaint the sign on several occasions. The final time this happened, Sanders found out. He and two visiting Shell district managers rushed down to the scene to stop Stewart's activities.

Sanders had previously threatened Stewart by saying he was going to "blow his god-damned head off" if he caught Stewart trying to repaint the sign again.

Upon the three men's arrival, Stewart jumped off his painting ladder and fired gun shots at the men. One of the Shell managers, Robert Gibson was killed. Gibson had been armed as well. Sanders took the weapon from Gibson's dead body and returned fire back at Stewart. Stewart was hit in the shoulder.

All of the men were arrested. Sanders and the surviving Shell manager were found not guilty.

Stewart was sentenced to eighteen years in prison for the murder of Gibson.

The only positive thing to come out of this gruesome experience is that Stewart's arrest for the murder eliminated any competition for Sanders' gas station.

At the age of forty five, Sanders was commissioned a Kentucky Colonel by the Governor of Kentucky. This was an honor afforded only to a few at the time. The Colonel's restaurant and service station continued to be a popular stopping point for tourists traveling through to Florida from the Northern part of the country.

By the end of the 1930's he would add a motel to his list of ever growing business ventures. But a fire soon destroyed it and his restaurant. Determined not to let this stop him, he would rebuild.

As the crisis of World War II gripped the nation, the tourist trade dried up and Sanders was forced to close his motel. The rationing of gasoline would add to the demise of the once flourishing enterprise. Colonel Sanders would spend the war years running

Government sponsored cafeterias. As the 1940's came to an end, Sanders had divorced his long time wife Josephine, and married his long time mistress Claudia who had helped him run his business ventures.

At the age of sixty two, (1952) Colonel Sanders sold the first set of rights to his chicken recipe to Peter Harman, who owned one of South Salt Lake City Utah's largest restaurants. He paid Sanders a few cents for every piece of chicken sold. During the first year, Harman's restaurant sales went up a considerable amount.

It would be a local sign painter who coined the phrase "Kentucky Fried Chicken". Harman liked the concept of "Southern Hospitality" especially all the way out in Utah. In time other local restaurant owners would join the new craze and pay the Colonel 4 cents a chicken for the use of the name and the secret herbs and spices.

Back in North Corbin Kentucky, the new Interstate 75 highway (part of the now famous Eisenhower highway system) severely reduced traffic to the restaurant in which Sanders still operated. He would go on to sell it outright at the age of sixty five. Once again circumstances beyond his control would force Colonel Sanders to move in a different direction. Like so many, a perceived set back would prove to open the door to a whole new world of fame and fortune for the now senior citizen.

After working so hard and for so long his entire life, Harland Sanders found himself in bad shape financially at the age of sixty five. In addition to his modest income from the few chicken royalties coming out of Utah, he only had a small savings and $105 a month in Social Security benefits. But the soon to be famous Kentucky Colonel was not done – far from it. He was convinced that his special chicken recipe would be popular all over the country. While his second wife ran a small restaurant in Shelbyville Kentucky, Sanders got in his car (with his now famous white suit and black tie outfit) and traveled across the country trying to convince restaurant owners to offer his Kentucky Fried Chicken to their customers. Each visit to a prospective restaurant was time consuming as the Colonel had to cook up his famous chicken as a demonstration. He often slept in his car to reduce expenses. He was on his way to age sixty six by this time.

The now famous founder of Kentucky Fried Chicken would be turned down hundreds of times by restaurant owners who doubted the value of Sanders' recipe. After persevering through hundreds of rejections, the idea began to catch on. Soon franchise prospects were coming to the Colonel to taste test his famous chicken.

Needless to say, the rest is history. By the 1960's Colonel Sanders was a cultural icon. There were KFC's practically on every corner in the nation. The tilted, spinning bucket that rotated in front of every store was true Americana. Sanders made appearances all over the United States and Canada for many years. People of all ages loved him, especially children. He had an almost Santa Claus like quality to him. He was now a multi millionaire. The one time broke senior citizen was now a national and cultural icon.

Sanders died in 1980 at the age of ninety.

Chapter Five:

Other Famous Failures

"I was cut by my High School basketball team. I went home and cried. I would go on to miss 9000 shots In my NBA career. On 26 occasions when I was being counted on to make the game winning shot, I missed".

- Michael Jordan

"I was told by a newspaper editor that I had no creative ideas. And my first animation company went bankrupt".

- Walt Disney

"We were told by an early record company that we were terrible and that guitar groups were on the way out. A concert promoter also told our manager to send any other group but us".

- The Beatles

"I was rejected by the University Of Southern California Film School twice".

- **Steven Spielberg**

"I struck out over 1300 times at bat during my career".

- **Babe Ruth**

"After the war ended, I was rejected for a job as an Engineer by Toyota Motors".

- Soichiro Honda

"My first book Carrie was rejected 30 times by publishers. In fact I wound up throwing it in the trash. My wife picked it out of the garbage and told me to keep going with it".

- Stephen King

"I failed in business 7 times before making it"

- R.H. Macy

"My cartoons were rejected by my high school year book".

- Charles Schultz

"We were plagued with problems and failure for years until one day we actually flew in the air".

- The Wright Brothers

Chapter Six:

Perspective

As we have studied the lives of these important people, it is clear that Life didn't single them out to be great from the start. All of them in their own way were met with stumbling blocks, notable setbacks and moments when they had to greatly doubt if they were ever going to achieve anything meaningful in life. Of the four subjects presented in this book, Abraham Lincoln stands out as the one who really should have given up long before he succeeded. For example, in his political career, Lincoln lost far many more elections to public office then he ever won. A more rational and reasonable person would have concluded that after that many defeats, politics was "just not for them".

But there was something in him that motivated his spirit to keep going despite suffering defeat on so many occasions. His is a great example of never giving up until a goal or task is accomplished.

And in light of such an example, here are some additional thoughts for all of us to ponder as we trudge the road of success and victory.

Positive Thinking As A Way Of Life - Not A Temporary Feeling

Over the years, I have attended, watched or listened to countless presentations by "motivational speakers" of many types and styles. A cliché of most motivational speakers today is to use high energy, a loud voice and create an atmosphere of "excitement" during the presentation. Their style is to get everyone so pumped up and motivated that they practically want to bust down the door of the auditorium on the way out. They feel ready to just take the world and its people by the tail. The newly motivated are determined to force others to conform to their will and determination to achieve their goals and desires.

One of the major problems with such an approach is that the high energy and motivation from a seminar only lasts a short time. It might last hours, days or maybe a few weeks. But for most people, life has a way of popping the air out of the motivation balloon. Life can dull even for the most determined devotees of temporary motivation. It's like eating your favorite candy bar. At first, it really feels great and tastes fantastic. The sugar high soon takes place and all seems well. But then the body has a way of metabolizing that sugar and often the inevitable "crash" takes place. Then the person is back to where they started and sometimes even further behind.

In defense of these "let's get all pumped up for an afternoon" experiences, there is often good information and an exposure to some powerful philosophies taught during these type of presentations that can have a lasting impact if absorbed and practiced as a way of life.

And this is where the power of positive thinking has its most strength – Making it a lifestyle.

The way we think is often a conscious decision. Sure, our minds are often like birds in a tree. Thoughts come and go, wisp in and out with little control on our part. But when we concentrate or seek to direct our minds, making the decision to choose positive and affirming thoughts versus self-defeating ones – that is when real change comes into peoples' lives.

Most of us are very familiar with the "glass half full" analogy. We have heard it for years. And even though it is well known, it has a real lesson in it for us upon closer examination.

This metaphor has real power even though it is so simple. It truly illustrates one's approach to life. Two different people can walk into a room and see the same glass of water sitting on a table. One can take joy and explain how awesome it is that the glass is fifty percent full and how much they could do with that. They could take a nice drink from it, water a plant or even wash a dish. The negative thinker immediately scoffs that only one half of the glass is full. In other words, fifty percent of the glass is empty, void of use and just a waste of space.

They further explain that what good is a glass that is designed to hold say two pints of fluid when only one pint is present? That person might be prone to just take the glass in hand and throw its contents into the sink. What they don't realize by doing that is that now the glass is one hundred percent empty and nothing can be done with it.

Think about it - the same glass on a table and two totally different interpretations. What's the difference? The difference is the decision of the person looking at it to see it a certain way.

The person who chooses to see life in the positive sees opportunity and what can be built from what already exists. The negative person – all they see if lack and emptiness. They focus on what's wrong – not what's right.

Another fun and great example of positive thinking as a way of life took place in the early American space program. One of the original astronauts was Gordon Cooper. His friends called him Gordo.

Gordo Cooper was one of the original seven astronauts chosen by the newly formed NASA in the late 1950's. The so called "space race" that unfolded during the 50's and 60's had much to do with the Cold War the United States was embroiled in with the Soviet Union. Conquering Space had more to do with each country's wish to gain superiority over the other in the eyes of the world.

An ongoing problem for the United States during this time was that the Soviet Union was way ahead in technological achievement.

It was this fact that prompted President John F. Kennedy to declare in 1961 that they United States was going to put a man on the moon and return him safely to Earth by 1970. Kennedy didn't seem to mind the fact that the United States had not even put a man into Earth orbit yet when he made his bold announcement. The Soviets had done so already a short time before Kennedy's speech.

The early American space flights were truly unprecedented and indeed very dangerous. Talk about positive thinking! All of the people associated with NASA during those years truly did have

"glass half full" attitudes.

Now back to Gordo Cooper. In 1963 Gordon Cooper was selected to command the "Faith 7", one of the early orbiting spaceships. John Glenn had been the first American to orbit the Earth the year before.

One of the goals of Faith 7 was to have the computers on board the spacecraft control the mission. In other words – NASA wanted a fully automated spaceship. The astronaut – Gordon Cooper was there simply for the ride – or to take over if something went wrong. Well a lot went wrong. And it was Gordon Cooper's "can do" attitude that saved his life and the mission. Gordo had orbited the Earth 22 times, more than any other astronaut up to that time.

Around orbit 19, the systems on board Faith 7 began to break down. The capsule had a power failure and the carbon dioxide level (the gas we release when we exhale) was building up in the space suit. This means that Cooper would be slowly running out of oxygen to breath. The interior temperature of the space craft was over 100 degrees. Due to the power failure, the onboard computers were not functioning. Cooper was forced to manually navigate by the stars. He had to use his wrist watch to time the firing of the re-entry rockets. And if his calculations were wrong, the small spaceship would burn up while re-entering Earth's atmosphere. And of course the "man in the can" would surely perish.

Recordings of Cooper's communication with NASA Mission Control still exist. In a calm and confident voice, Gordo Copper is heard saying something to the equivalent of....

"Well things are starting to stack up a little bit. The ACS inverter is acting up and my carbon dioxide is building up in the suit, the navigation computer is dead, the electrical panels are dead - nothing will come on line... but other than that, things are fine".

Other than that – everything is fine!

Now there is a man with a life style of a positive mental attitude.

The good news is that due to his amazing technical skill and training, Gordon Cooper was able to manually bring his spacecraft back to Earth and landed in the ocean closer to the awaiting aircraft carrier than any previous spaceship had done.

Gordon Cooper's example of working with what was right with a situation and not focusing on all the problems around him is a wonderful lesson to us all.

There will be times when even the most dedicated positive thinker will get off track and "fall off the wagon". The sometimes harsh circumstances of life can get even the most ardent person discouraged and feeling like it's time to throw in the towel. But time and time again we have seen that the person who chooses positive thinking as a life style will get back on their feet, dust off the road dirt and press on.

Seeing the glass half full is a mental and emotional decision not a temporary feeling.

When You Think It's Totally Over – It's Not!

Who among us has not had a tremendous disappointment or a let-down after a monumental amount of time, emotional investment and overall effort was put into a project or goal? Most of us have had that experience and it can be devastating. A failure after exerting a huge amount of blood, sweat and tears into something can leave us bitter and broken.

And during the initial phases after the collapse of our goal or dream, we are usually convinced that our hopes.... well are now hopeless. The dream is over – the pieces of our shattered efforts can never be glued back together again. We feel like Humpty Dumpty. The failure that we experienced was on such a grand scale that we just know in our hearts that our hope is gone forever.

But the lessons of history have a funny way to once again prove us wrong. Ironically, the story of politics is wonderfully helpful to us in turning away from hopelessness and despair. Its lessons are so profound and inspiring.

And here is a very important one........

Of course we covered the political failures of Abraham Lincoln in a previous chapter. Anyone in their right mind would have gotten out of politics if they had failed and/or lost as many elections as he did. But nonetheless we know that he persevered into iconic greatness.

But we do not have to go back as far as Lincoln to see this lesson appear again.

For most of the 1950's Richard Nixon was the Vice President of the United States under Dwight D. Eisenhower. Today of course, Nixon is best known as the disgraced President brought down by the Watergate scandal of the 1970's. But back then

Nixon was a respected former member of Congress and Ike's "right hand man".

1960 would be Eisenhower's last year in office. After Franklin Roosevelt's death, Presidents were limited to two consecutive terms. The popular F.D.R. had been actually been elected 4 times and died in office during 1945. Being an ambitious man, Nixon decided to run for President in 1960 – to follow and continue the popular and prosperous Eisenhower years.

Few people were positioned better than Nixon that year for a run at the Presidency. Of course there was another ambitious fellow who had his eye on the White House in 1960 and his name was John F. Kennedy, a popular Senator from Massachusetts.

Both men campaigned tirelessly. Nixon in fact made it a goal to personally visit all 50 states during the campaign. Day after day, night after night, Nixon and Kennedy crisscrossed this nation making speeches, shaking hands and kissing babies.

Any citizen who has witnessed a Presidential election year cycle can only conclude that the process is an exhausting and grueling task for the participants.

Finally it was Election Day 1960. Both Kennedy and Nixon had done all they could to convince voters that they were the best choice to lead the United States into the 1960's.

Over sixty eight million votes were cast. The popular vote was split almost right down the middle. Each man got just over thirty four million votes each. In fact the popular vote was so close that Kennedy had only 112,000 more votes than Nixon. Out of over sixty eight million votes!

As an aside, historians have often questioned the "official" results of the election. Cities like Chicago under the famous Mayor Richard J. Daley may have given JFK a little more "help" when the final tallies were counted.

But regardless Richard Nixon conceded the election and John F. Kennedy became the President Elect of the United States.

Those of us who have never been through such an experience can hardly imagine the physical and emotional toll that such a loss must take on a person. Nixon would go on to run for Governor of California two years later but was defeated again.

In 1962 Nixon held a very historic press conference shortly after his California defeat. He lambasted the press corps and ended the speech by saying "You won't have Nixon to kick around anymore".

Every political pundit would have bet his bottom dollar that Richard Nixon's political career was over.

But clearly it was not. Nixon spent the ensuing years making speeches and continuing to network with party bosses.

It was now 1968, eight years after his crushing defeat. John Kennedy was now dead, having been assassinated five years earlier in 1963. JFK's brother Robert was running for President also in 1968, trying to capture the Democratic nomination. But sadly he too was cut down by gun fire in June.

It was a very hard fought election. 1968 was a very challenging year. Both Martin Luther King and Robert Kennedy had been murdered within a few months of each other. The youth protests over the Vietnam War were growing and getting very unruly. President Johnson was deeply unpopular. And at the Democratic Convention in Chicago, the police were beating protestors in the street right in front of the Convention's hotel. And it was broadcasted daily on national television.

Finally in November, 1968 Nixon won the Presidency. The Democratic nominee, Hubert Humphrey had only 511,000 fewer votes than Nixon. But Nixon had a huge Electoral College victory over Humphrey.

After a humiliating defeat in 1960 to Kennedy and 1962 (Governor), Richard Nixon was now the President of the United States.

Before Watergate set in, Nixon would go on to accomplish many great things as President – notably, putting the final imprint on ending the Vietnam War, opening up relations with China and the development of the Environmental Protection Agency (EPA).

Nixon is a stunning example and study of great defeat and ultimate victory. His perseverance and determination changed not only his life but the history of this country.

Chapter Seven:

Life Lessons

It's been a fascinating journey studying the lives of these iconic Americans. Time and time again, we have seen them come from less than desirable circumstances and rise to greatness -and after much adversity and failure. And while the four subjects of this book had many different problems in which to overcome, it is clear that ultimately they all had the following character traits that propelled them to their places in history.

- **They had a vision:** The men outlined in this book all had an idea where they wanted to go before they started and never let it go. They faltered, got off track and were delayed in achieving their goals, sometimes for years. But with the aid of today's twenty/twenty hindsight, it is clear that they all got back up even after being knocked over again and again.

- **Past circumstances didn't define them:** Each subject had their own unique backgrounds and challenges. Some were dirt poor, had very limited education and others suffered personal tragedy at young ages. And in spite of these circumstances, these men consistently saw the future as a blank slate. They never allowed the colors of their past to paint the canvas of their futures. In other words, the past really had no connection to their future achievements. They had no ties to prior limitations. In the end it was as if the past had never existed.

- **They never ever gave up:** This one trait truly is the most important of them all. History has shown that time and time again people who have reached a goal or an ultimate achievement did so because they would not allow themselves to give up. They might have gotten discouraged and given up temporarily, but in the end, they got back on the grind wheel and stayed with it until they succeeded. If there is one message that could be conveyed to all young people today, the lesson of persistence would truly be the most important of them all.

In the end, it is clear that life plays no favorites. Maybe for some, there are temporary advantages, but ultimately life itself is the great equalizer. The truly great news is that all of us can be an Edison, Ford, Lincoln and Sanders. The moment when we truly believe that we are no different from any other human being when it comes to the rules of "making it" the hard part will be over.

It's all been done before. All we need to do is imitate the greats of history by having a vision and making a concerted effort. Add in the ability to reflect on mistakes and the willingness to learn from them. And top it all off with good old fashioned persistence. And before we know it, we will marvel at how little time it took to achieve the desires of our heart.

"PEOPLE NEVER FAIL, THEY JUST STOP TRYING"

- HENRY FORD

Further Reading and Study

- "The Strangest Secret" - Audio Recording by Earl Nightingale, 1956.

- "Think and Grow Rich" - by Napoleon Hill, 1937.

- " How to Win Friends and Influence People" - by Dale Carnegie, 1936.

- "How I Went from Failure to Success In Selling" - by Frank Bettger, 1947.

- "Success Through A Positive Mental Attitude" - by Napoleon Hill and W. Clemont Stone, 1960.

58947634R00050

Made in the USA
Charleston, SC
22 July 2016